THE MIRACULOUS POWER

OF THE

ROSARY

HARNESSING THE STRENGTH OF MARY'S INTERCESSION

REV. FR. JOHN COLLINS

TABLE OF CONTENTS

INTRODUCTION

CHAPTER ONE
- The history and significance of the Rosary

CHAPTER TWO
- The power of Mary as an Intercessor

CHAPTER THREE
- The benefits of the Rosary for Mental and Emotional well-being

CHAPTER FOUR
- The rosary and the power of intercession

CHAPTER FIVE
- The Rosary and personal spiritual growth

CHAPTER SIX
- The Rosary and family life

CHAPTER SEVEN
- The Rosary and personal Transformation

CHAPTER EIGHT

- The Rosary and community building

INTRODUCTION

Have you ever wondered about the true power of the rosary? The simple repetition of prayers and beads has been a staple of Catholic devotions for centuries, but few people realize the full extent of its transformative effects. In "The Secret Strength of the Rosary", we will delve into the mysterious and miraculous world of this ancient practice. From personal testimonies to historical accounts, you will discover the hidden secret behind the rosary and the ways in which it can change your life. Whether you are a seasoned rosary devotee or simply curious about its power, this book will open your eyes to the wonders of this humble prayer practice. Get ready to unlock the full potential of the rosary and experience the peace, strength, and grace that comes with it.

Throughout the book, you will learn about the various elements of the rosary and their symbolism, as well as the rich history and cultural significance of this devotion. You will also gain a deeper understanding of the role of Mary, the mother of Jesus, in our lives and her power as an intercessor. With a mix of inspiring stories and practical tips, "The Secret Strength of the Rosary" will guide you on a journey to a deeper spiritual life and help you harness the power of ancient prayer practice.

Additionally, the book will explore the ways in which the rosary can help with personal struggles such as anxiety, depression, and fear, as well as provide comfort and peace during difficult times. You will discover the power of the rosary to heal physical, emotional, and spiritual wounds, and find guidance on how to use the rosary in your daily life.

Whether you are looking for a way to deepen your faith, find inner peace, or just explore the mysteries of this ancient prayer, "The Secret Strength of the Rosary" is the perfect guide. With its inspiring stories and practical wisdom, this book will help you tap into the full potential of the rosary and bring you closer to God.

CHAPTER ONE

THE HISTORY AND SIGNIFICANCE OF THE ROSARY

The rosary is a beloved devotion among Catholics and has been practiced for centuries. It is a form of prayer that involves the repetition of prayers and the use of beads as a physical aid to keep count. But the rosary is much more than just a simple prayer practice - it has a rich history and cultural significance that has made it an integral part of the Catholic faith.

The origins of the rosary can be traced back to the late 12th century. According to tradition, the rosary was introduced by Saint Dominic, a Spanish priest who used the devotion as a way to combat the spread of Albigensianism, a heretical movement that was sweeping Europe at the time. Saint Dominic believed that the repetition of prayers and meditation on the lives of Jesus and Mary would be a powerful tool in the fight against heresy and would help people to deepen their faith.

Over time, the rosary became widely popular, and it wasn't long before it was embraced by the Church as an official devotion. In the 13th century, Pope Innocent III declared the rosary a form of devotion that was approved by the Church. From that point on, the rosary became an integral part of Catholic worship, and it continues to be an important part of the faith today.

The significance of the rosary can be seen in its ability to bring people together in prayer and to deepen their spiritual lives. The repetition of prayers and meditation on the lives of Jesus and Mary helps to focus the mind and to quiet the heart, allowing people to connect with God on a deeper level. The rosary also provides a sense of comfort and peace in difficult times, and it has been used as a tool of healing and transformation for centuries.

In addition to its spiritual benefits, the rosary is also a way to honor Mary, the mother of Jesus. Mary plays an important role in the Catholic faith, and the rosary provides an opportunity to reflect on her life and her role as a mediator between God and humanity. Through the repetition of prayers and meditation on her life, Catholics can deepen their relationship with Mary and seek her intercession.

The rosary has also played an important role in the history of the Catholic Church. It has been used as a tool of spiritual warfare, as well as a source of comfort and solace during times of political and religious unrest. It has also been embraced by many spiritual leaders, including saints and popes, who have encouraged its use as a way to deepen one's spiritual life.

The rosary has also had a cultural impact, and it has been an important part of Catholic worship for centuries. The devotion is practiced all over the world, and it is a way for Catholics to connect with each other, regardless of race, ethnicity, or cultural background. The rosary is also an important part of many Catholic traditions, including Marian feasts and processions, and it continues to be a beloved devotion among Catholics today.

In conclusion, the rosary is a powerful devotion that has a rich history and cultural significance. Its ability to bring people together in prayer, deepen spiritual lives, and provide comfort and peace has made it an integral part of the Catholic faith. Whether you are a seasoned rosary devotee or just exploring this ancient prayer practice for the first time, the history and significance of the rosary will inspire and enlighten you on your journey to deeper faith and spiritual growth

CHAPTER TWO

THE POWER OF MARY AS AN INTERCESSOR

The Catholic faith teaches that Mary is the mother of Jesus and the mother of all believers. She holds a special place in the hearts of Catholics, and her role as an intercessor is an important part of the rosary devotion. Through the repetition of prayers and meditation on her life, Catholics seek Mary's intercession, asking her to pray for them and to help them deepen their relationship with God.

The idea of Mary as an intercessor can be traced back to the early days of the Church, when the apostles and early Christians turned to her for support and comfort. Mary's role as an intercessor was further developed over time, and by the Middle Ages, she was widely recognized as the mother of all believers and a powerful mediator between God and humanity.

The power of Mary as an intercessor is rooted in her relationship with God. As the mother of Jesus, she was privileged to share in the life of the Son of God and to receive special graces from God. Her close relationship with Jesus gives her a unique understanding of his love and mercy, and her role as an intercessor allows her to share that love and mercy with all of us.

The rosary is a powerful tool for seeking Mary's intercession. The repetition of prayers and meditation on her life allows

Catholics to connect with Mary on a deeper level and to seek her help in their spiritual journey. Mary's intercession can bring comfort and peace in difficult times, and it can help Catholics to deepen their relationship with God and to grow in their faith.

- The intercession of Mary can also help us to better understand and appreciate the love of God. Through the repetition of prayers and meditation on her life, we are reminded of God's great love for us and the lengths to which he is willing to go to save us. Mary's intercession helps us to see God's love more clearly and to feel it more deeply in our own lives.

The rosary is also a way to honor Mary and to show our love and gratitude for her. The repetition of prayers and meditation on her life allows us to reflect on her life and her role as a mediator between God and humanity. We can also use the rosary to ask for Mary's help and to seek her guidance as we navigate the challenges of life.

The power of Mary's intercession is not limited to Catholics, and her intercession is sought by believers of many different Christian denominations. Mary is also venerated by many other religious traditions, and her role as an intercessor is widely recognized across many cultures and traditions.

In conclusion, Mary's role as an intercessor is an important part of the Catholic faith and the rosary devotion. Her close relationship with God and her love for all of us make her a powerful mediator between God and humanity. Through the repetition of prayers and meditation on her life, Catholics can seek Mary's intercession and find comfort, peace, and spiritual growth on their journey of faith. Whether you are Catholic, Protestant, or of another faith tradition, the rosary is a devotion that can help you to deepen your relationship with God and to experience his love more deeply. So why not pick up a rosary today and begin your journey of faith? The power of this ancient devotion is waiting for you.

CHAPTER THREE

THE BENEFITS OF THE ROSARY FOR MENTAL AND EMOTIONAL WELL-BEING

The rosary has a lot of benefits for your Mental, Emotional Well-Being.

In addition to its spiritual benefits mentioned earlier, the rosary can also have a positive impact on our mental and emotional well-being. Through the repetition of prayers and meditation on Mary's life and the lives of the saints, we can find comfort, peace, and solace in our lives. The rosary can also help us to manage stress, reduce anxiety, and overcome feelings of sadness and depression.

The rosary is a form of mindfulness meditation that allows us to focus on the present moment and to quiet our minds. By repeating prayers and meditating on Mary's life, we can shift our focus away from our problems and worries and towards the love and peace of God. This can help to calm our minds and to reduce stress and anxiety.

The rosary can also provide comfort in times of sadness and depression. The repetition of prayers and meditation on Mary's life can remind us of God's love and care for us, and can help us to find hope and comfort in difficult times. The rosary can also help us to cultivate a positive outlook and to see the good in life, even in the midst of challenging situations.

The rosary is also a form of spiritual exercise that can help us to grow in our faith and to deepen our relationship with God. Through the repetition of prayers and meditation on Mary's life, we can learn more about our faith and the lives of the saints, and we can also develop a closer relationship with God. This can have a positive impact on our mental and emotional well-being, helping us to feel more connected and fulfilled in our lives.

The rosary can also provide a sense of comfort and security. By repeating the prayers and meditating on Mary's life, we can feel the love and protection of God and of Mary. This can help to ease any fears or anxieties that we may have and bring a sense of peace and security to our lives.

The rosary can also be used as a form of prayerful reflection. By meditating on each mystery, we can reflect on our own lives and the ways in which we can imitate the virtues and actions of Mary and the saints. This can help to bring a sense of clarity and purpose to our lives and can help us to live our lives more fully and with greater meaning.

Incorporating the rosary into our daily routine can also bring us a sense of inner peace and stability. The repetitive nature of the prayers can serve as a grounding force, helping to bring a sense of calm and stillness to our thoughts and emotions. By focusing on the prayers, we can let go of any distractions or worries and focus on the present moment. This can help to reduce stress and bring a sense of peace and contentment to our lives.

Finally, the rosary can be a source of inspiration and encouragement. As we repeat the prayers and meditate on the lives of Mary and the saints, we can draw strength and inspiration from their examples of faith, courage, and love. This can help us to persevere in our own lives, even in the face of challenges and difficulties.

In conclusion, the rosary is a powerful tool for improving our mental and emotional well-being. Through the repetition of prayers and meditation on Mary's life, we can find comfort, peace, and solace in our lives, manage stress and anxiety, and overcome feelings of sadness and depression. Whether you are facing difficult times or simply seeking to deepen your relationship with God, the rosary is a powerful devotion that can help you to find the peace and happiness you seek.

CHAPTER FOUR

THE ROSARY AND THE POWER OF INTERCESSION

The rosary is not only a powerful tool for personal spiritual growth, but it can also be used for the benefit of others through intercession. Intercession is the act of praying for others, and the rosary is one of the most effective forms of intercession due to its focus on Mary and the saints.

One of the key benefits of intercession is that it can help us to develop a sense of compassion and care for others. By praying for those in need, we can feel a sense of connection with them and can offer them love and support. This can help us to develop a deeper sense of empathy and understanding for others, and can help us to see the world from a different perspective.

Intercession can also be a source of comfort for those in need. By knowing that others are praying for them, those in need can feel a sense of love and support, even in the midst of difficult situations. This can help to ease their worries and anxieties, and can bring them a sense of peace and comfort.

It is also important to note that intercession through the rosary can be done for anyone, regardless of their religion or beliefs. The power of prayer transcends all boundaries, and the rosary can be a powerful tool for promoting unity and understanding between people of different backgrounds and beliefs. By praying for others, we can help to break down barriers and promote a sense of commonality and understanding.

Another important aspect of intercession is the power of intention. When we pray the rosary, it is important to have a specific intention in mind. This can be for someone in need, for peace in a particular area, or for a specific cause. By focusing our prayers on a specific intention, we can help to bring about the change that we desire, and can experience the power of the rosary in a more tangible way.

The rosary can also be a tool for self-intercession. By using the rosary to pray for ourselves, we can experience personal growth and healing. This can help us to overcome challenges and difficulties, and can help us to grow in our relationship with God and with

In addition to its personal benefits, intercession can also have a powerful impact on the world. By praying for peace, justice, and harmony, we can help to bring these qualities to our communities and to the world at large. The rosary can be a powerful tool for promoting change and for bringing about a more just and peaceful world.

Finally, intercession can be a way of connecting with Mary and the saints. By praying for others through the rosary, we can feel the presence of Mary and the saints and can experience their love and care for us. This can help to deepen our relationship with Mary and the saints, and can help us to feel more connected to the larger community of faith. It is important to remember that intercession through the rosary is a communal effort. The rosary is not just about personal growth and change, but about the power of community and the power of prayer. By praying the rosary together with others, we can experience the power of intercession in a more profound way, and can help to create a sense of community and

In conclusion, the rosary and the power of intercession are a powerful combination. By using the rosary to pray for others, we can experience personal growth, offer comfort and support to those in need, and help to bring about positive change in the world. So why not add the power of intercession to your rosary practice today and experience the difference it can make in your life and in the lives of others?

CHAPTER FIVE

THE ROSARY AND PERSONAL SPIRITUAL GROWTH

The rosary is not only a powerful tool for intercession, but it can also be a tool for personal spiritual growth. The repetition of the prayers and the focus on the mysteries of the life of Jesus and Mary can help to deepen our relationship with God and with Mary, and can help us to grow in our faith.

One of the key benefits of the rosary is its ability to quiet the mind and promote reflection. By repeating the prayers and focusing on the mysteries, we can let go of our worries and distractions, and can allow ourselves to enter into a state of deep reflection and contemplation. This can help us to connect with God and to experience a sense of peace and calm.

The rosary can also be a powerful tool for spiritual growth because it helps us to focus on the life of Jesus and Mary. By meditating on the mysteries, we can deepen our understanding of their lives and can gain a greater appreciation for their teachings and examples. This can help us to grow in our faith and to live more fully in accordance with the teachings of Jesus and Mary.

In addition to its many benefits for personal spiritual growth, the rosary can also help us to develop a closer relationship with Mary. Mary is a powerful intercessor and can help us to grow in our faith and our relationship with God. By focusing on her life and her role as the mother of Jesus, we can gain a greater appreciation for her teachings and examples, and can experience her love and care in a more tangible way.

In order to get the most out of the rosary and to experience its full benefits for personal spiritual growth, it is important to approach it with a spirit of reverence and devotion. This means taking the time to reflect on the mysteries, to enter into a state of deep contemplation, and to allow ourselves to be fully present in the moment.

It is also important to approach the rosary with an open heart. By letting go of our worries and distractions, and by allowing ourselves to be open to the love and care of God and Mary, we can experience the full benefits of the rosary and can grow in our faith and our relationship with God.

Finally, the rosary can be a way of connecting with the larger community of faith. By praying the rosary with others, we can experience the power of community and can feel a sense of connection with others who are also seeking to deepen their relationship with God.

In conclusion, the rosary and personal spiritual growth are closely linked. By using the rosary to deepen our relationship with God and to grow in our faith, we can experience a sense of peace and calm, gain a greater appreciation for the teachings of Jesus and Mary, and feel a sense of connection with the larger community of faith. So why not make the rosary a regular part of your spiritual practice and experience the difference it can make in your life?

CHAPTER SIX

THE ROSARY AND FAMILY LIFE

The rosary can also be a valuable tool for strengthening the bonds of family and promoting harmony within the home. By praying the rosary together, families can experience the power of community and can feel a sense of connection with one another.

The rosary can help families to focus on their faith and to live more fully in accordance with the teachings of Jesus and Mary. By meditating on the mysteries and reflecting on the life of Jesus and Mary, families can deepen their understanding of their faith and can gain a greater appreciation for the values and teachings that they hold dear.

Praying the rosary together can also help to create a sense of peace and calm within the home. By taking time to focus on their faith and to connect with God and Mary, families can experience a sense of peace and calm that can help to alleviate stress and tension, and can promote greater understanding and harmony within the home.

In addition, the rosary can be a source of comfort and support for families. By repeating the prayers and meditating on the mysteries, families can experience the love and care of God and Mary, and can feel a sense of connection and comfort even in difficult times.

It's important to delve deeper into the practical ways in which families can incorporate the rosary into their daily lives. Here are some suggestions for ways to make the rosary a regular part of your family's spiritual practice:

1. Set aside a specific time for rosary each day. This can be after dinner, before bed, or another time that works best for your family. By having a set time for the rosary, it can become a routine and an important part of your family's day.
2. Assign a different family member to lead each decade of the rosary. This can help to keep everyone engaged and involved, and can provide an opportunity for each family member to take a leadership role.
3. Use visual aids, such as rosary beads or a rosary chart, to help children understand the prayers and the mysteries. These can also be a helpful way to keep everyone on track and to stay focused during the rosary.
4. Encourage quiet reflection and contemplation during the rosary. Turn off electronic devices, minimize distractions, and create a peaceful environment to help everyone focus on the prayers and the mysteries.
5. Consider incorporating different types of rosary meditations or variations, such as the Divine Mercy Chaplet or the Sorrowful Mysteries, to keep the rosary fresh and interesting for everyone.

Incorporating the rosary into your family's daily life can be a wonderful way to deepen your faith, to strengthen the bonds of family, and to promote a sense of peace and calm in your home. By following these suggestions and making the rosary a regular part of your family's spiritual practice, you can experience the many benefits of this powerful prayer.

Finally, the rosary can be a way of connecting families with the larger community of faith. By praying the rosary together with others, families can experience the power of community and can feel a sense of connection with others who are also seeking to deepen their relationship with God.

In conclusion, the rosary can be a valuable tool for strengthening the bonds of family and promoting harmony within the home. By praying the rosary together, families can experience the power of community, deepen their understanding of their faith, and experience a sense of peace and comfort even in difficult times. So why not make the rosary a regular part of your family's spiritual practice and experience the difference it can make in your home and family life?

CHAPTER SEVEN

THE ROSARY AND PERSONAL TRANSFORMATION

The rosary can also be a powerful tool for personal transformation and spiritual growth. By meditating on the mysteries and repeating the prayers, individuals can deepen their relationship with God and can experience a sense of peace, comfort, and renewal.

One of the key benefits of the rosary is that it provides an opportunity for quiet reflection and contemplation. By taking time to focus on the prayers and the mysteries, individuals can gain a deeper understanding of their faith and can experience a sense of connection with God.

In addition, the rosary can help individuals to work through their challenges and struggles. By repeating the prayers and meditating on the mysteries, individuals can find comfort and support, and can gain a greater appreciation for the love and care of God and Mary.

The rosary can also be a source of inspiration and motivation. By reflecting on the life of Jesus and Mary and the lessons they teach us, individuals can be encouraged to live more fully in accordance with their faith and to strive to be their best selves.

It's also important to talk about the different ways in which individuals can use the rosary for personal growth and transformation. Some suggestions include:

1. Incorporating different themes or intentions into each decade of the rosary. For example, one decade can be focused on gratitude, another on healing, and another on peace. By focusing on different themes each day, individuals can gain a deeper understanding of these important aspects of their lives and can experience a greater sense of peace and well-being.
2. Using the rosary as a form of spiritual journaling. Write down any thoughts or insights that come to mind while praying the rosary. This can be a great way to reflect on your spiritual journey and to track your progress over time.
3. Reflecting on the lives of the saints. Consider incorporating the lives of the saints into your rosary meditations. Read about their lives, their challenges, and their successes, and let their stories inspire and encourage.
4. Combining the rosary with other spiritual practices, such as meditation or yoga. This can help to deepen the spiritual experience and to enhance the benefits of the rosary.
5. Praying the rosary in different settings, such as in nature, at a church, or at a shrine. This can help to keep the rosary fresh and interesting and can provide a greater sense of connection to the larger community of faith.

By incorporating these different approaches into your rosary practice, you can experience the full range of benefits that this powerful prayer has to offer. The rosary has the power to transform lives and to bring peace, comfort, and renewal. So why not make it a regular part of your spiritual practice and see for yourself what it can do for you?

Finally, the rosary can be a way of connecting with the larger community of faith. By praying the rosary with others, individuals can experience the power of community and can feel a sense of connection with others who are also seeking to deepen their relationship with God.

In conclusion, the rosary can be a powerful tool for personal transformation and spiritual growth. By taking time to pray the rosary and to reflect on the mysteries, individuals can deepen their relationship with God, work through their challenges, find inspiration and motivation, and connect with the larger community of faith. So why not make the rosary a regular part of your spiritual practice and experience the difference it can make in your life?

CHAPTER EIGHT

THE ROSARY AND COMMUNITY BUILDING

The rosary can also play an important role in building and strengthening communities of faith. By praying the rosary together, individuals can experience the power of community and can feel a sense of connection with others who share their beliefs and values.

One of the key benefits of praying the rosary in community is that it provides a sense of solidarity and support. When individuals come together to pray, they can feel a sense of belonging and can experience the comfort and encouragement that comes from knowing that others are praying for the same intentions.

Praying the rosary in community can help to foster a greater sense of understanding and respect among individuals who may come from different backgrounds or who may have different perspectives on life. By sharing a common prayer, individuals can find common ground and can build relationships based on mutual respect and understanding.

Another benefit of praying the rosary in community is that it can help to promote peace and harmony. By coming together in prayer, individuals can experience a sense of unity and can work towards resolving conflicts and promoting understanding.

There are many different ways to incorporate the rosary into community building activities. For example, communities can organize regular rosary events, such as a monthly rosary walk, or a weekly rosary gathering. Communities can also organize rosary retreats, which provide individuals with the opportunity to spend a day or a weekend focused on prayer and reflection.

It is also worth mentioning that the rosary is not only a tool for building community within one's own religious group, but it can also serve as a bridge between different religious communities. The rosary is a devotion that is shared by people of different Christian denominations, as well as by people of different faith traditions.

For example, many Catholic communities organize ecumenical rosary events, which bring together individuals from different Christian denominations to pray together. These events provide an opportunity for individuals to come together in a spirit of unity and respect, and to build relationships across religious divides.

The rosary can be a powerful tool for promoting peace and understanding between different religious communities. For example, communities can organize inter-faith rosary events, which bring together individuals from different faith traditions to pray together. These events provide an opportunity for individuals to learn about one another's beliefs and values, and to build relationships based on mutual respect and understanding.

Finally, communities can use the rosary as a way to reach out to others who are in need. For example, communities can organize rosary events for individuals who are struggling with illness, grief, or other challenges. These events can provide a source of comfort and support for individuals who are in need, and can help to build stronger relationships within the community.

In conclusion, the rosary can play an important role in building and strengthening communities of faith. By praying the rosary together, individuals can experience the power of community, foster greater understanding and respect, promote peace and harmony, and reach out to others who are in need. So why not make the rosary a regular part of your community building activities and see the positive impact it can have?

Printed in Great Britain
by Amazon